RONALDO

Abbeville Press Publishers

New York · London

A portion of the book's proceeds are donated to the **Hugo Bustamante AYSO Playership Fund,** a national scholarship program to help ensure that no child misses the chance to play AYSO Soccer. Donations to the fund cover the cost of registration and a uniform for a child in need.

Text by Illugi Jökulsson

For the original edition
Design and layout: Ólafur Gunnar Guðlaugsson

For the English-language edition
Editor: Joan Strasbaugh
Production manager: Louise Kurtz
Designer: Ada Rodriguez
Copy editor: Ken Samuelson

PHOTOGRAPHY CREDITS

Getty Images
1. Champions: Shaun Botterill. 4. Practicing the free kick: Angel Martinez. The free kick: Chivas/CON. 24–25. Ronaldo weeps: Claudio Villa. Ronaldo with the cup: Jeff J Mitchell. 28–29. Ronaldo and Irina Shayk: Denis Doyle. Ronaldo Jr.: Jasper Juinen. 30–31. Free kick: Chivas/CON. 46 and 47. Celebration: Denis Doyle. 48–49. Advertisement: GAMMA. 50–51. Ronaldo celebrates: David Ramos. Ronaldo training: Jasper Juinen. Strength training: Chinaphotopress. Backflip penalty kick: Denis Doyle. The free kick: Laurence Griffiths. Injured: Denis Doyle. 46–47. Celebration: Denis Doyle. 54–55. Rally: Europa Press. Audi: Juan Naharro Gimenez. 62. Celebration: Dennis Doyle.

Shutterstock
Front cover and back cover
4, 6, 7, 8, 9, 10, 11, 12, 13, 14, 15, 17, 18, 19, 20, 21, 22, 23, 26, 27, 32, 33, 34, 35, 40, 41, 42, 43, 44, 45, 52, 53, 54, 55, 56, 57, 59

36. Ronaldo að skalla/**Árni Torfason.**

All statistics current through the 2012–2013 season unless otherwise noted.

First published in the United States of America in 2014 by Abbeville Press, 137 Varick Street, New York, NY 10013

First published in Iceland in 2012 by Sögur útgáfa, Fákafen 9, 108 Reykjavík, Iceland

First edition
10 9 8 7 6 5 4 3 2 1

Library of Congress Cataloging-in-Publication Data

Illugi Jvkulsson.
  [Cristiano Ronaldo. English]
  Ronaldo / by Illugi Jvkulsson. — First edition.
      pages cm. — (World soccer legends)
  Translated from Icelandic.
  Summary: "The story of the "ultimate footballer," Cristiano Ronaldo. Covers the star's youth in Madeira, his nicknames, his record with Manchester United, and includes a list of the numerous awards he has received"—Provided by publisher.
  ISBN 978-0-7892-1166-8 (hardback)—ISBN 0-7892-1166-1 (hardcover) 1. Ronaldo, Cristiano, 1985—Juvenile literature. 2. Soccer players—Portugal—Biography—Juvenile literature. I. Illugi Jvkulsson. Cristiano Ronaldo. Translation of: II. Title.
  GV942.7.R626I45 2014
  796.334092—dc23
  [B]
                          2013045842

For bulk and premium sales and for text adoption procedures, write to Customer Service Manager, Abbeville Press, 137 Varick Street, New York, NY 10013, or call 1-800-ARTBOOK.

Visit Abbeville Press online at **www.abbeville.com.**

CONTENTS

The Ultimate Player	8
Where Does He Come From?	10
CR's Birthday	12
Three Ronaldos!	14
The Beginning in Portugal	16
Manchester, England!	18
How Tall Is He?	20
Favorites	22
United and Ronaldo	24
Triumphs and Tribulations	26
Playing for United 2003–2009	28
Family Man	30
Lethal Free Kicks	32
Portugal's Three Heroes	34
Captain of Portugal!	36
The Boss	38
To Real Madrid!	40
Ronaldo's Strengths	42
Ronaldo and Real	44
Spanish Champion!	46
The Best!	48
Wanted!	50
10 Facts	52
How Much Does He Make?	54
Serious Car Lover!	56
What Next?	58
Learn More! / Glossary	60
The Ronaldo Board Game!	62

THE ULTIMATE

Alex Ferguson, former Manchester United manager

"I think he's the best player in the world. He can play with both feet, he has fantastic skill, strength, and bravery, and he's a great header of the ball. I saw how he dedicated himself in training sessions to becoming the best in the world."

José Mourinho, Chelsea coach

"Cristiano Ronaldo is unique. Each year he achieves such great accomplishments that you think that he can't do better. But then he always improves. He's simply on another level than other footballers."

PLAYER

Where Does He Come From?

Cristiano Ronaldo comes from Funchal, the largest town on the island of Madeira, which belongs to Portugal.

Portugal

The country covers an area of 35,500 square miles in total and has a population of 10.5 million. The capital is called Lisbon and has 550,000 inhabitants.

The Madeiras

The largest island, Madeira, is 286 square miles and has a population of 260,000, of which 111,000 live in the capital, Funchal. Twenty-seven miles away is another island, Porto Santo, which is 16 square miles in size and has a population of 4,300. There are several smaller, uninhabited islands in the archipelago. The islands are roughly 300 miles off the coast of Africa, and more than 620 miles from the mainland of Portugal. The flight between Madeira and Lisbon takes approximately one-and-a-half hours. The Madeiras are 250 miles north of the Canary Islands, which belong to Spain.

History

European ships sailing along the African coast probably found the Madeiras a long time ago, and around AD 1420 sailors and merchants from Portugal started to settle on them. The Portuguese cleared the forests that covered the islands in order to plant sugarcane. The sugar plantations were later moved to Brazil and replaced with vineyards. There is a variety of wine produced in the archipelago called Madeira wine. In addition to agriculture, the islanders

MADEIRA

Funchal

Portugal

make their living from fishing, tourism, and financial services.

In 1976, the Madeiras were granted political autonomy.

Soccer

Soccer is the most popular sport in Portugal. The three strongest clubs by far are Benfica and Sporting from Lisbon, and Porto from the city of Oporto. Porto has dominated the Portuguese League since the beginning of the 21st century. In recent years, the club Braga has been growing in strength. There are several soccer clubs in Madeira, and two of them, Maritimo and Nacional, play in the Portuguese top division. They are among the strongest clubs in the league and have competed in the European tournament, but haven't won any trophies or titles. Matches between these two teams are heated affairs.

Who is he?

Cristiano Ronaldo is the youngest of four siblings. He has one older brother, Hugo, and two older sisters called Elma and Liliana Catia. They are considerably older than him, as they were born between 1974 and 1976.

Ronaldo's parents were called José Dinis Aveiro and Maria Dolores dos Santos, and were regular working-class people. José was a gardener and Dolores a cook. The family had very little money to spare.

What is his name?

One of his sisters got to choose his first name, but his middle name was inspired by Ronald Reagan, who was president of the United States when Ronaldo was born. Reagan used to be a modestly successful film star and was a favorite of Ronaldo's father.

According to Portuguese naming traditions, people usually use the surnames of both mother and father, so the boy's full name is . . .

Cristiano Ronaldo dos Santos Aveiro.

CR's Birthday

Cristiano Ronaldo was born on February 5, 1985. His zodiac sign is Aquarius, which reigns in the sky from January 21 to February 19. Of course, astrology has no scientific value, but people born in the zodiac sign of Aquarius are said to be fit, frank, diligent, energetic, and imaginative. That would certainly describe Cristiano Ronaldo! Body parts ruled by Aquarius are the thighs, ankles, feet, and chest—that also seems about right! The name Aquarius, which means "water-bearer" or "cup-bearer," comes from Greek Greek mythology. The Aquarius was a boy called Ganymede who was known for being the greatest and most handsome in the world. Cristiano would probably say that sounded just about right, too!

He shares his birthday with other famous soccer heroes. Two of those are retired: Gheorge Hagi, an incredible midfielder from Romania who played with both Real Madrid (1990–1992) and FC Barcelona (1994–1996), and Giovanni van Bronckhorst, who was a left back for Barcelona (2003–2007) and played more than 100 internationals for the Netherlands.

Two of the best strikers active today also share a birthday with Ronaldo. The Argentine Carlos Tévez was born on February 5, 1984, and the Brazilian Neymar was born on February 5, 1992. Barcelona's Neymar will probably compete with Cristiano Ronaldo for the media's attention during the next few years!

Finally, a hugely promising young midfielder with Manchester United, the Belgian Adnan Januzaj (of Kosovar-Albanian ethnicity), was born on February 5, 1995.

A Good Day for Soccer!

February 5
Hagi 1965
Bronckhorst 1975
Tévez 1984
C. Ronaldo 1985
Neymar 1992
Januzaj 1995

Three Ronaldos!

The name Ronaldo is not very common, so it's a little strange that three men all named Ronaldo have been elected World Player of the Year a total of six times in thirteen years.

THE FIRST RONALDO

Ronaldo Luis Nazário de Lima, Brazil
Born on September 18, 1976

Ronaldo

Ronaldinho

The greatest goal machine in the world from 1995–2005, he scored countless goals for PSV Eindhoven, Barcelona, Inter Milan, and Real Madrid. He suffered frequent injuries but was completely unstoppable when he was in top form. Ronaldo was fantastic with the Brazilian national team, was elected FIFA World Cup Best Player in 1998, and was awarded the Golden Shoe in the 2002 World Cup. He holds the record for most goals scored in a World Cup Final, a total of 15.

From 1993–2011, Ronaldo played 518 matches with his clubs and scored 387 goals. He played 98 internationals and scored 62 goals.

He was awarded the FIFA World Player of the Year in 1996, 1997, and 2002 as well as the Ballon d'Or in 1997 and 2002! The two awards were combined, in 2010.

LITTLE RONALDO!

Ronaldo de Assis Moreira
"Ronaldinho," Brazil
Born on March 21, 1980

He emerged while Ronaldo Nazário was still in his prime and so he was dubbed "Ronaldinho," or "Little Ronaldo," to distinguish between the two. Ronaldinho played with Barcelona from 2003 to 2008. At his best he was incredibly skilled, tricky, and entertaining to watch on the field. He was an amazing scorer and some of his free kicks were simply breathtaking. Ronaldinho contributed greatly to his national team, and both Ronaldo Nazário and Ronaldinho were on the 2002 World Cup team. Eventually Ronaldinho seemed to lose interest in playing for the big European clubs, and he moved back to Brazil in 2011.

As of fall 2013, Ronaldinho had played a total of 675 club matches and scored 265 goals. He had also played 97 internationals and scored 33 goals. He was awarded the FIFA World Player of the Year in 2004 and 2005 and the Ballon d'Or in 2005!

FIFA Ballon d'Or (World Player of the Year until 2009)

Year	Player	Year	Player
1991	Lothar Mattäus	2003	Zinedine Zidane
1992	Marco van Basten	2004	Ronaldinho
1993	Roberto Baggio	2005	Ronaldinho
1994	Romário	2006	Fabio Cannavaro
1995	George Weah	2007	Kaká
1996	Ronaldo	2008	Ronaldo
1997	Ronaldo	2009	Lionel Messi
1998	Zinedine Zidane	2010	Lionel Messi
1999	Rivaldo	2011	Lionel Messi
2000	Zinedine Zidane	2012	Lionel Messi
2001	Luís Figo		
2002	Ronaldo		

What does the name mean?

"Ronaldo" is the same name as "Ronald" in English. It is Nordic in origin and means "he who rules with counsel" or "wise ruler."

THE BEST RONALDO?

Three years after Ronaldinho was elected FIFA World Player of the Year, it was CRISTIANO RONALDO's turn. He was awarded the honor in 2008.

The defining talents of Ronaldo Nazário were speed and explosive power. Ronaldinho was known for his feints, sly passes, and beautiful free kicks. It's fair to say that Cristiano Ronaldo combines the best talents of the two earlier Ronaldos!

When will the next Ronaldo appear?

Cristiano Ronaldo

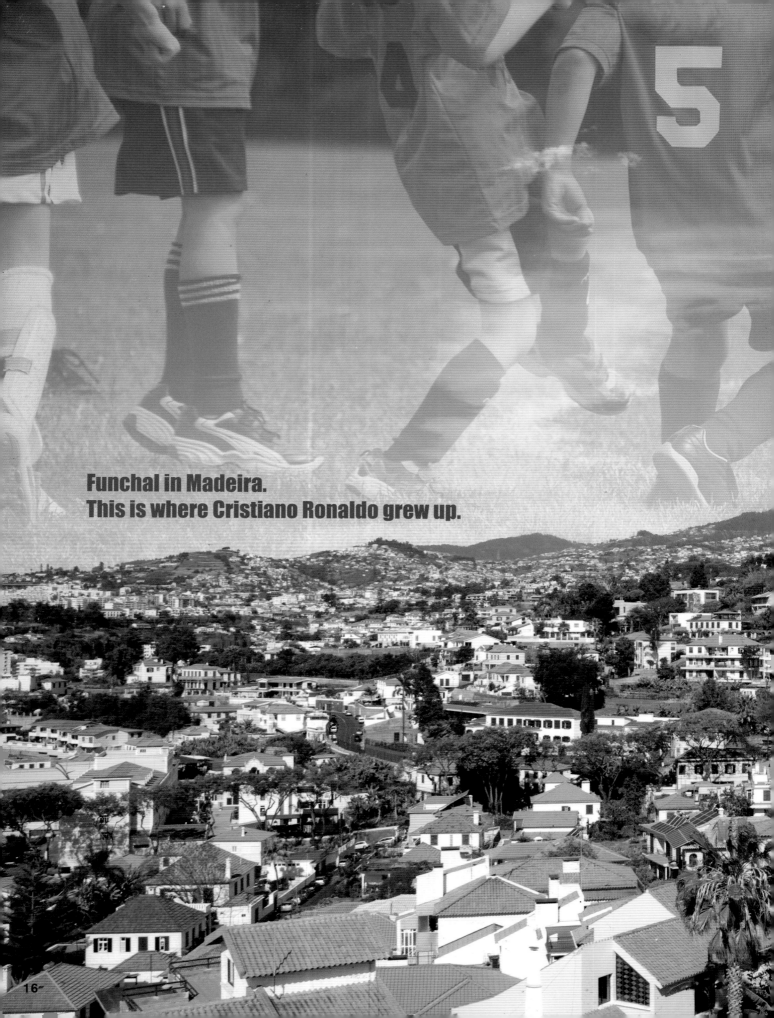

Funchal in Madeira.
This is where Cristiano Ronaldo grew up.

The Beginning in Portugal

Cristiano Ronaldo's father, José Dinis Aveiro, was a soccer fan. He took care of the uniforms for the soccer club Andorinha, which is a small club in Santo António—the neighborhood in Funchal where Ronaldo grew up. José gave his son a soccer ball for his fifth birthday, and Ronaldo loved it so much that he even took it to bed with him! Ronaldo's mother Dolores also supported him wholeheartedly when she and her husband realized that their boy was unusually talented at soccer.

He played in the youth teams for Andorinha but joined a larger club in Funchal, Nacional, when he was 10. By then, anyone could see that Cristiano Ronaldo would go far. He was extremely talented but also hardworking and ambitious. Nobody was more conscientious at training. He would get very upset if things didn't go well; sometimes he would break down in tears and his teammates would laugh at him. He didn't care—he was just so determined to do well and to WIN!

When he was just 12 years old, Sporting, one of the biggest Portuguese clubs, bought him from Nacional. In that day and age, it was unheard of that a mighty club in Lisbon would pay so much for a 12 year old, but the management of the club was convinced that he would become one of soccer's greats. It was a big step for a small kid who had never left Madeira to move to Lisbon by himself. At first, Ronaldo was often lonely and missed his family. But he dealt with it by training harder, determined to become the world's best player!

On October 7, 2002, Ronaldo debuted with Sporting's first team in the Portuguese Premier League. The opposing club was Moreirense. Ronaldo was 17, and he started with a bang. The youngster scored two goals in the match, which Sporting won 3–0.

The first goal was a taste of what was to be expected from Ronaldo. After passing back and forth with his teammate in midfield, Ronaldo took off with the ball, leaving all of Moreirense's midfielders and defenders in the dust. He made a fine scissor move as he whizzed past the remaining defenders and smashed the ball under the goalkeeper and into the net. Cristiano Ronaldo had arrived on

MANCHESTER, ENGLAND!

This photo of Cristiano Ronaldo and Steven Gerrard celebrating a goal for Liverpool . . . and this one of Ronaldo celebrating a goal for Arsenal are both fakes! But actually, they could have been real. In the autumn of 2002, Ronaldo was invited to train with Arsenal. Arsenal's manager, Arsene Wenger, is known for having a great eye for young talent, but somehow he didn't spot Cristiano Ronaldo! In the spring of 2003, Ronaldo's agents offered him to Liverpool, and the Merseyside club certainly was interested. It was obvious that the lad had potential! But eventually Liverpool's manager,

Gerard Houllier, decided that Ronaldo was too young. He felt that Ronaldo needed to mature and play a bit longer at home in Portugal. So he turned down the offer. That was a huge sporting and business blunder if there ever was one!

Sir Alex swoops in

The English soccer superpower Manchester United visited Lisbon in the summer of 2003 to play a practice match against Sporting, which Cristiano Ronaldo played for at the time. He was just 18. Even though United was one of the great clubs of European soccer, Sporting won the match 3–1. Ronaldo was the key to the team's success. He outplayed United's players time and again. There are several versions of what happened next.

One story goes that on the way to the airport after the match, the United players Rio Ferdinand and Ryan Giggs sat down on the bus next to the manager, Alex Ferguson. They were fascinated by the young Portuguese player and almost ordered their manager to buy him for United. Sir Alex agreed and shouted to the bus driver to turn around. They drove back to Sporting headquarters and Ferguson signed Ronaldo there and then.

It may not have happened exactly like this, as in all probability United had already decided to buy Ronaldo before going to Portugal. But it is true that he impressed everyone with his skill, and that was the last game he played for Sporting. Soon enough he was on a plane headed for Manchester.

Return to Portugal

In September 2007, four years after Ronaldo left Sporting, the two clubs met again in Lisbon, in a UEFA Champions League match. It was on the very same field where Ronaldo had played with Sporting against United in that practice match. Sporting had a strong team and they were determined to win on their home ground. But they failed to score, and when the match was almost over, Ronaldo scored an unexpected header.

He seemed to be slightly uncomfortable scoring that vital goal against his old club. After modestly celebrating the goal with his teammates in United, he bowed to the Sporting fans. He had been their idol. And when the match ended with a 1–0 victory for United, the Sporting supporters gave their lost son a standing ovation. He had entertained them so much in the past that they generously forgave him for crushing their hopes of victory.

HOW TALL IS HE?

Cristiano Ronaldo grew tall at an early age.
He's 6 foot 1 and 186 lbs.

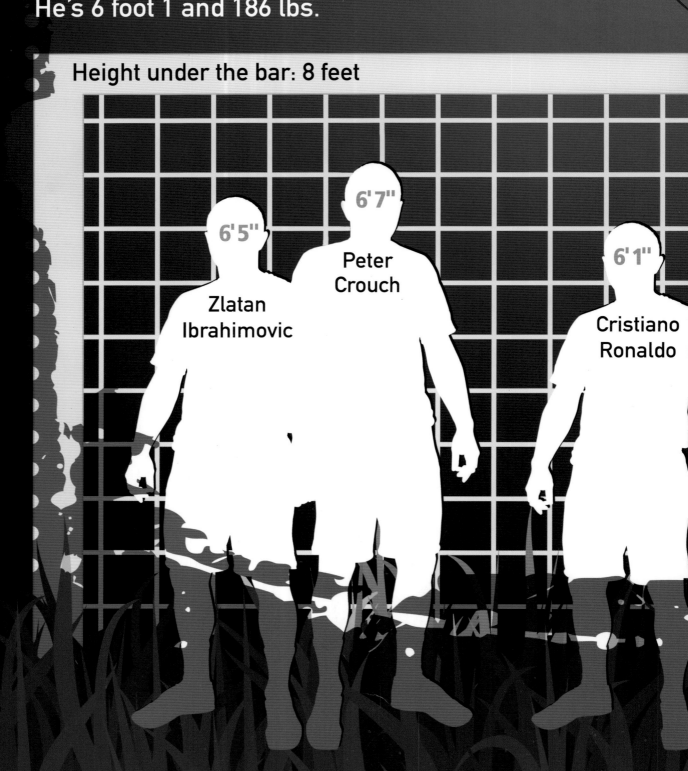

Height under the bar: 8 feet

6' 5"

Zlatan
Ibrahimovic

6' 7"

Peter
Crouch

6' 1"

Cristiano
Ronaldo

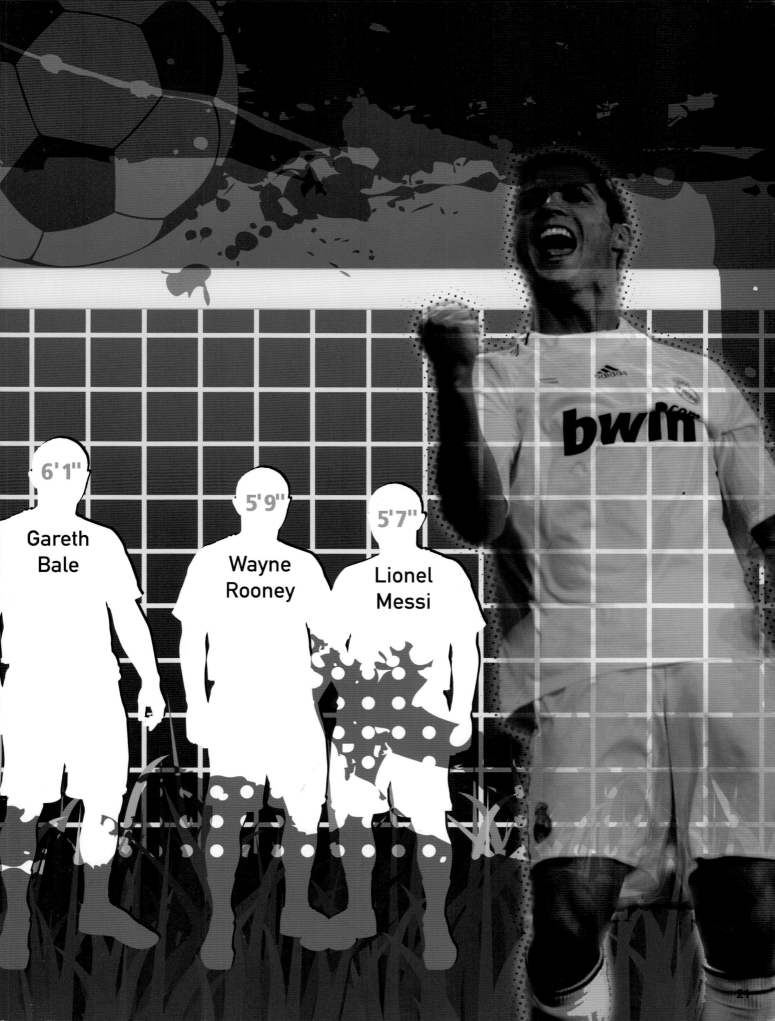

6'1"

Gareth
Bale

5'9"

Wayne
Rooney

5'7"

Lionel
Messi

Favorites

Favorite Food:
Bacalao!

Salt fish—or bacalao as it's called—is very popular in both Spain and Portugal. The fish is salted cod caught in northern waters, especially around Iceland. The Portuguese have hundreds of bacalao recipes, and one of them is "Bacalhau à Brás." It's really easy to make, and it's available all over Portugal, almost like fast food.

Ronaldo enjoyed this dish often when he was growing up in Madeira, and he says that Bacalhau à Brás is still his favorite food!

Cook Ronaldo's Favorite Meal!

Bacalhau à Brás

21 oz. bacalao
olive oil
3 onions, thinly sliced
2 cloves of garlic, finely chopped
18 oz. potatoes, shredded
6 eggs, beaten
salt and pepper to taste

Sauté the onion and garlic in the olive oil in a large pan. Cut the cod into long strips, and shred the potatoes so they resemble matchsticks. Add the fish to the pan and, while it fries, deep-fry the potato sticks in another pan. When the potatoes are ready add them to the pan with the fish, and gently stir all the ingredients together. Then beat the eggs in a bowl with a fork and pour them onto the pan. Stir gently until the eggs are cooked. Serve and eat!

Favorite Drink: Santal fruit drink.

Favorite Music: Romantic music by Sade, George Michael, Elton John, and Phil Collins. Any kind of dance music. "When I need to get my eyes open in the morning, I listen to

George Michael

catchy Brazilian music!" he claims.

Nicknames: *Cry-Baby*, when he was young and would often break down when things didn't work out. *Little Bee*

(*Abelinha*), because he was such a hard worker. Teammates in Real Madrid call him *Máquina,* which means machine, because of his relentless training. Also often referred to as *CR7*.

Lucky Charm: White rosary.

Best Qualities: He is very lively and focused.

Faults: He can be stubborn and sometimes a bit petty.

What he won't forgive: Betrayal.

UNITED and Ronaldo

Cristiano Ronaldo scored his first goal for United on November 1, 2003. He took a free kick from the far left flank, and the ball soared across the field, dropping suddenly into the back of the net. In the spring of 2004, he scored the first goal for United in the FA Cup Final, when United beat Millwall 3–0.

Aside from these goals, Ronaldo didn't score much during his first seasons with United. He was young and had obvious potential, but he could be slightly unreliable. Sometimes he seemed to drift off, and he was often accused of diving and was too prone to complaining to the referee.

But, he wasn't meant to be a top scorer in those first seasons, anyway. Manager Sir Alex Ferguson felt he was best positioned on the flank. But Ronaldo improved each year, becoming stronger and more confident. His goal-scoring abilities proved to be phenomenal, anywhere on the field. In the 2007–2008 season, he was no longer just promising, but simply one of the best players in the world.

Season	League matches	League goals	Total matches	Total goals
2003–2004	29	4	40	6
2004–2005	33	5	50	9
2005–2006	33	9	47	12
2006–2007	34	17	53	23
2007–2008	34	31	49	42
2008–2009	33	18	53	26

Premier League 2003–2004

1 **Arsenal**
2 Chelsea
3 Manchester United

UEFA Champions League: Round of 16, lost to Porto under the management of José Mourinho. Porto went on to win the title that year. **Ronaldo goals: 0**

Premier League 2004–2005

1   Chelsea
2   Arsenal
3   Manchester United

UEFA Champions League: Round of 16, lost to AC Milan. Liverpool won the title. **Ronaldo goals: 0**

Premier League 2005–2006

1   Chelsea
2   Manchester United
3   Liverpool

UEFA Champions League: Disaster. Number four in their preliminary group. Barcelona won the title. **Ronaldo goals: 1**

Premier League 2006–2007

1   Manchester United
2   Chelsea
3   Liverpool

UEFA Champions League: Lost in the semi-final to AC Milan, who went on to defeat Liverpool in the final. **Ronaldo goals: 3**

Premier League 2007–2008

1   Manchester United
2   Chelsea
3   Arsenal

UEFA Champions League: United defeated Chelsea in the final in Moscow. The match concluded with a 1–1 draw. Ronaldo scored the United goal with a header. Frank Lampard scored for Chelsea. In the penalty shoot-out, Petr Chech saved a penalty kick from Ronaldo, but United still won in the end. **Ronaldo goals: 8**

Premier League 2008–2009

1   Manchester United
2   Liverpool
3   Chelsea

UEFA Champions League: United made it to the final the second year running, but lost 2–0 to Barcelona. Samuel Eto'o and Lionel Messi scored the goals. **Ronaldo goals: 4**

TRIUMPHS AND TRIBULATIONS

With Manchester United, Ronaldo achieved all the greatest victories there are on the field. But he also had to endure disappointments. In the smaller photo, he is celebrating the 2007–2008 UEFA Champions League title with teammate Wayne Rooney. The match against Chelsea was held in Moscow. In the larger photo, Ronaldo is walking brokenhearted off the field after losing the Champions League final the following year. That match was played in Rome, and Barcelona beat United 2–0. In the background is the victorious coach of the Catalan team, Pep Guardiola.

CRISTIANO RONALDO

WITH MANCHESTER UNITED
2003–2009

CHIEF AWARDS AND HONORS

ENGLISH PREMIER LEAGUE
2007, 2008, 2009

FA CUP 2004

FOOTBALL LEAGUE CUP 2006, 2009

FA COMMUNITY SHIELD 2007

FIFA CLUB WORLD CUP 2008

UEFA CHAMPIONS LEAGUE
2008

PREMIER LEAGUE GOLDEN
BOOT 2007–2008

UEFA CHAMPIONS LEAGUE
TOP SCORER 2007–2008

BALLON D'OR 2008

FIFA PUSKÁS AWARD
FOR THE MOST BEAUTIFUL
GOAL 2009

Playing for United

2003–2009
The first season

Cristiano Ronaldo played 40 matches during his first season with United, 2003–2004, and usually came off the bench.

Goals 2003–2004
(all competitions)

1. Rudd van Nistelrooy 30
2. Paul Scholes 14
3T. Diego Forlán, Ryan Giggs 8
5. Louis Saha 7
6. Cristiano Ronaldo 6

ManU's starting eleven usually looked like this during Ronald's first season:

Tim Howard

O´Shea – Silvestre

G. Neville   P. Neville

Scholes – Keane – Fortune – Giggs

Van Nistelrooy – Forlán

The final season

One year after Ronaldo joined United, Sir Alex bought an 18-year-old striker from Everton, Wayne Rooney. And the team changed little by little. In 2008–2009, Carlos Tévez also played a lot in the front line. He and Cristiano Ronaldo share the same birthday (see p. 13). A friend of Ronaldo's from Portugal, Nani, joined United in 2007–2008 and played alongside him.

(see p. 13)

Goals 2008–2009

(all competitions)

1. Cristiano Ronaldo 26
2. Wayne Rooney 20
3. Carlos Tévez 15
4. Dimitar Berbatov 14
5. Nemanja Vidic 7

ManU's starting eleven usually looked like this during Ronaldo's last season:

Van der Sar

Ferdinand – Vidic

O'Shea · · · · · · · · · · · Evra

Ronaldo – Fletcher – Carrick – Giggs

Rooney – Berbatov

Family Man

Cristiano Ronaldo's father, José Dinis Aveiro, was very proud of his son and of his success as a soccer player. He would visit him in Manchester on a regular basis and watch him play. When everything was fine, they had a really good relationship.

But things weren't always fine; José was an alcoholic and drank too much. It was very difficult for those around him, and the drinking also ruined his health.

When Ronaldo was all grown up, he made several attempts to help his father and get him therapy, but to no avail. José was too afflicted by his alcoholism.

On September 7, 2005, Ronaldo was in Moscow with the Portuguese national team. The upcoming match was Russia–Portugal in the 2006 World Cup qualifiers. Ronaldo was just 20 years old but already one of Portugal's brightest stars.

Shortly before the match, coach Felipe Scolari and captain Luis Figo approached Ronaldo. They told him as gently as they could that his father had died. He had succumbed to alcohol-related liver failure.

Ronaldo was devastated. Scolari and Figo told him that of course he would not have to play against Russia, but Ronaldo insisted. He wanted to play in honor of his father and try to score a goal for him.

He didn't score a goal in that particular match, but the next time he scored a goal for Portugal he dedicated it to his father.

A risk not worth taking

It was not only Ronaldo's father who had to battle addiction. His older brother Hugo has struggled with both alcohol and drug addiction.

Hugo managed to kick the habit with Ronaldo's help. Ronaldo is a sensible man; he knows that if your parents or close family members have struggled with addiction, you may well be vulnerable too. He doesn't want to risk falling prey to alcoholism, and therefore he decided at an early age never to drink alcohol.

José Dinis

He takes this vow very seriously and once sued an English paper for claiming that he had been drinking. It turned out to be untrue. Cristiano Ronaldo doesn't drink.

Dolores Aveiro with little Cristiano.

Romance and parenthood

Cristiano Ronaldo is a handsome young man, and he has been in several relationships with beautiful women. Since moving to Madrid, he has been in a relationship with the Russian model Irina Shayk, who is, however, not the mother of his son.

His son? Oh yes! He has a son! To everyone's surprise, Ronaldo announced in July 2010 that he had fathered a child. He broke the news on his Facebook page. There, Ronaldo claimed to feel "great joy and emotion" over the birth of his son. Nobody knows who the boy's mother is, because, according to Ronaldo, she doesn't want to be in the spotlight. He also announced that he would have full custody of the boy, who was given the name Cristiano. What else?!

Ronaldo's mother Dolores and his sisters have helped him in raising little Cristiano.

Cristiano Ronaldo and Irina Shayk

Lethal

Ronaldo is the complete player. Like most world-class strikers, he can score any type of goal, but his right foot is his main weapon.

Ronaldo's free kicks have always been lethal. His specialty is the long-range "tomahawk" free kick, as he has dubbed it. His explosive power is so great that sometimes the opponent's goalkeeper hardly manages to move.

Ronaldo is always very focused before he takes the kick. He thrusts the ball deep into the grass and takes his stance with eyes locked on target. His stance, with his legs apart, is easily recognizable. He then runs very deliberately towards the ball and FIRES!

Of his many amazing free kicks, the very best is probably the goal he scored against Portsmouth on January 30, 2008. It was a thirty-yard screamer that was so powerful that goalkeeper David James hadn't even moved when the ball thrust into the net. And even if James had managed to respond, it's highly unlikely that he could have defended the goal. The recordings showed not only the incredible force of the shot but also that the ball changed direction slightly on its thunderous way to the goal—twice!

Free Kicks

Ronaldo's goals 2011–2012

Header	6
Free kick	4
Penalty kick	14
Right foot	26
Left foot	9

Portugal's Three Heroes

Three Portuguese players have been among the very best, each in his era.

EUSÉBIO

On the national team 1961–1973

Eusébio

Eusébio was a fantastic goal scorer. He played for Benfica in Lisbon for 15 years, scoring a total of 473 goals in 440 appearances for the club. And he scored 41 goals in his 64 internationals.

Eusébio was called the "Black Pearl," "Black Panther," or simply "o Rey"—the King. He was born in Mozambique, which was under Portuguese rule at the time. His father came from Angola, another Portuguese colony.

Almost singlehandedly, Eusébio led the Portuguese team to the bronze medal of the 1966 World Cup in England, where he scored 9 goals! Eusébio was widely revered for his elegant play, fairness, and humility.

Though popular on the home front, Cristiano Ronaldo has yet to achieve Eusébio's level of popularity in Portugal, perhaps due to the fact that Ronaldo has spent most of his career abroad.

FIGO

On the national team 1991–2006

Figo started his career with Sporting Lisbon, just like Ronaldo. He played as a superbly gifted winger or playmaker. In 1995, he went to Barcelona and was twice Spanish champion with the club. In 2000, he crossed over to Real Madrid, causing outrage among Barcelona fans. When he returned to Camp Nou in the Real shirt, someone threw a piglet's head onto the

Figo

field to shame Figo for his "betrayal." He became champion twice with Real, and won the 2001–2002 UEFA Champions League. He was awarded the Ballon d'Or in 2000.

Figo is the most capped player for Portugal of all time, having appeared in 127 international matches. It's highly likely that Ronaldo will break that record. As Figo himself said, "If I'd been born with Ronaldo's talent, I wouldn't have had to work so hard."

CRISTIANO RONALDO

On the national team since 2003

Cristiano Ronaldo (top right), captain of the Portugal national team, before a match against Poland in 2012.

Captain of Portugal!

Cristiano Ronaldo played his first match for Portugal on August 20, 2003. He was 18 years old and had recently transferred to Manchester United. The match was a friendly against Kazakhstan. The young Ronaldo started on the bench but came on at halftime.

The UEFA Euro 2004 was hosted by Portugal. The hosts were determined to win, and they had a strong and talented team. Figo was one of the best attacking midfielders in the world, and other strong players were Couto on defense, midfielder Rui Costa, and the forwards Nuno Gomes and Pauleta.

At the end of August 2013, he had played 105 internationals, scoring 40 goals.

The coach, Luiz Felipe Scolari, had Ronaldo up his sleeve and intended to use the lightning-quick young winger as his secret weapon. As it turned out, Ronaldo played a great deal, and was soon on the starting eleven. It was, however, a great disappointment for Portugal when they lost in the final to Greece. It was an unexpected and unfair result. Greece played a gritty defensive game but managed to net one goal. Try as they might, Ronaldo and the other Portuguese attackers didn't manage to score an equalizer.

Portugal played well in the 2006 World Cup

qualifiers, and Ronaldo was nothing short of spectacular, scoring 7 goals. When the finals began in Germany on June 9, 2006, Portugal did well to begin with. They beat England in the quarterfinals in a penalty shoot-out, after a 0–0 draw in extra time. Ronaldo secured the win for Portugal. But then Portugal lost to France in the semifinals, and again to the Germans in the match for third place. The World Cup was therefore a disappointment for both Portugal and Ronaldo.

The 2008 European Championship didn't go well for Portugal, either. Ronaldo had scored 8 goals in the qualifiers, and Portugal made it to the semifinals, where they were eliminated by Germany. Ronaldo was starting to feel the heat from fans.

The disappointment continued in the 2010 World Cup. The new coach, Carlos Queiroz, appointed Ronaldo as captain. At first, this didn't seem to do either the team or Ronaldo any favors. He didn't score a single goal in the qualifying campaign, and Portugal almost didn't make it to South Africa. There, Portugal underperformed, though they did thrash the weak North Korean team 7–0. (Ronaldo scored his one and only goal in this match.) After two 2–2 draws, Portugal was eliminated from the competition by Spain in the round of 16.

After a bad start, Portugal made it to the finals of Euro 2012 in Poland and the Ukraine. There Ronaldo showed his mettle. He led his men to a good win over Denmark and then scored both goals as Portugal defeated the Dutch 2–1. In the quarterfinals, the inspirational captain then scored the winning goal against the Czech Republic. Portugal had reached the semifinals, but then they were defeated on penalties by the eventual winners, Spain.

What will he achieve in Brazil 2014?

Tournaments	Matches	Goals
2004 Euro	6	2
2006 FIFA World Cup	6	1
2006 Euro	3	1
2010 FIFA World Cup	4	1
2012 Euro	5	3

Unsportsmanlike?

Ronaldo played superbly in the 2006 FIFA World Cup, even though he didn't score many goals. However, there was a lot of controversy around one incident in a match against England. Wayne Rooney, Ronaldo's United teammate,  stamped on the foot of one of the Portuguese defenders. Ronaldo loudly complained to the referee, who obligingly sent Rooney off. In replays of the incident, Ronaldo could be seen winking at his Portuguese teammates.

The referee later clarified that his decision had not been based on Ronaldo's complaining but on the severity of Rooney's foul. That did not appease the English supporters, who blamed Ronaldo for England's elimination from the World Cup. And of course hated him for it!

At this time, Ronaldo was often criticized for diving and various theatrics. But Rooney came to his teammate's defense claiming that he'd done nothing wrong, and eventually the English fans forgave him.

THE BOSS

Cristiano Ronaldo's talent is so great it would have emerged wherever his career took off. But he was extremely fortunate in ending up at Manchester United, where manager Sir Alex Ferguson knew exactly how to handle him. He eased Ronaldo into his team, without ever putting too much pressure on him. At the same time, he made it clear that he had the utmost confidence in the young Portuguese.

When Ronaldo arrived at Old Trafford, he asked for the shirt number 28, the number he had worn at Sporting. But Ferguson insisted he should have number 7, which had previously been used by such United legends as George Best, Bryan Robson, Eric Cantona, and David Beckham.

Ronaldo said, "The famous shirt was an extra source of motivation. I was forced to live up to such an honor."

And he certainly did.

Ferguson became a sort of father figure to the young forward. When Sir Alex Ferguson finally retired in 2013, his former protégé tweeted simply but gracefully:

"Thanks for everything, Boss."

Manchester United manager Sir Alex Ferguson gives instructions to Cristiano Ronaldo during the UEFA Champions League Group F match against AS Roma at Old Trafford in Manchester, England, on October 2, 2007.

Cristiano Ronaldo @Cristiano
Thanks for everything, Boss. pic.twitter.com/WfU1h2Prhb   8 May
🔲 Hide photo   ↩ Reply   ⇄ Retweet   ★ Favorite   ☑ Pocket   ••• More

100,015 RETWEETS   **44,063** FAVORITES

11:12 AM - 8 May 13 · Details

Flag media

To Real Madrid!

Early on, people started to discuss a possible transfer for Cristiano Ronaldo from Manchester United to Real Madrid of Spain. It seemed almost inevitable at some point, as Real is one of the very strongest clubs in the world. Ronaldo had always longed to play for the team.

In the summer of 2009, Ronaldo felt it was time to leave, and Sir Alex Ferguson, manager of Manchester United, was willing to let him go. He knew that for his protégé the Real dream was simply too strong to resist.

Ronaldo was grateful and said, "He has been like a father to me in the sport and one of the most important factors and most influential in my career."

Real paid United 93.9 million euros for Ronaldo, making him the most expensive soccer player in history.

The most expensive players up to 2014:

1 Gareth Bale, Wales
Tottenham to Real Madrid 2013
100 million euros

2 Cristiano Ronaldo, Portugal
ManU to Real Madrid 2009
94 million euros

3 Zinedine Zidane, France
Juventus to Real Madrid 2001
75 million euros

4 Zlatan Ibrahimovic, Sweden
Inter Milan to Barcelona 2009
69 million euros

5 Kaká, Brazil
AC Milan to Real Madrid 2001
68 million euros

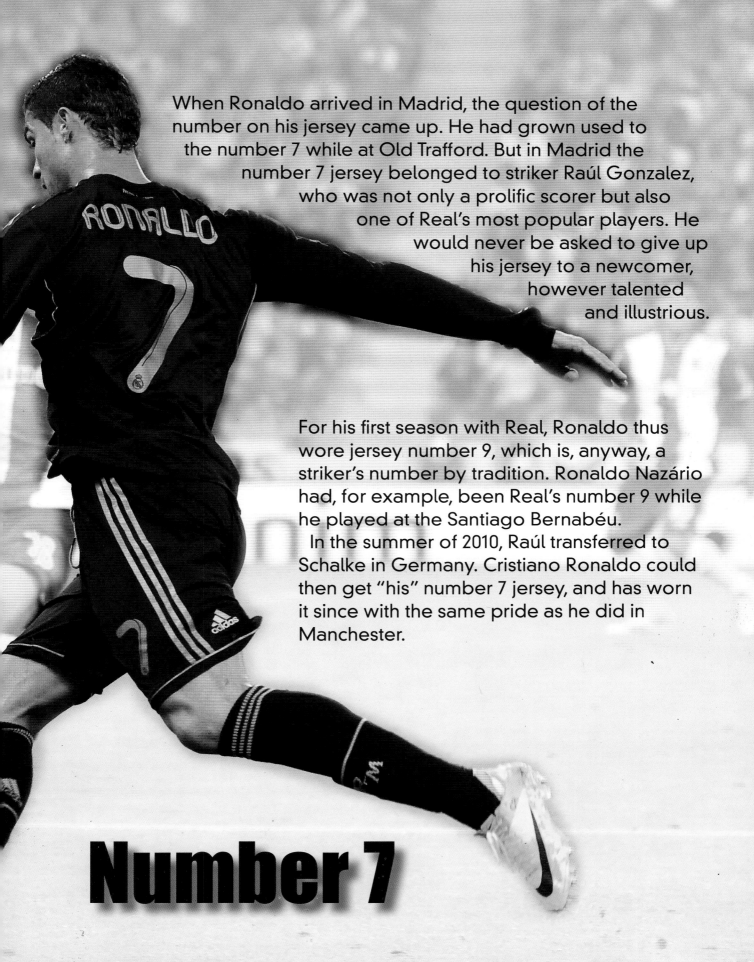

When Ronaldo arrived in Madrid, the question of the number on his jersey came up. He had grown used to the number 7 while at Old Trafford. But in Madrid the number 7 jersey belonged to striker Raúl Gonzalez, who was not only a prolific scorer but also one of Real's most popular players. He would never be asked to give up his jersey to a newcomer, however talented and illustrious.

For his first season with Real, Ronaldo thus wore jersey number 9, which is, anyway, a striker's number by tradition. Ronaldo Nazário had, for example, been Real's number 9 while he played at the Santiago Bernabéu.
  In the summer of 2010, Raúl transferred to Schalke in Germany. Cristiano Ronaldo could then get "his" number 7 jersey, and has worn it since with the same pride as he did in Manchester.

Number 7

Ronaldo's Strengths

Eidur Gudjohnsen

Before a match between Real Madrid and Barcelona in April 2012, BBC Sport asked the Icelandic player, Eidur Gudjohnsen, to compare the stars of the two teams, Cristiano Ronaldo and Lionel Messi. Gudjohnsen knows both players well, having played against Ronaldo several times while they were both in the Premier League—Ronaldo with United and Gudjohnsen with Chelsea—and then having played with Messi at Barcelona. Here is what Gudjohnsen had to say about Ronaldo.

Technique
His stepover is legendary. Rarely have we seen a player of such skill, at such speed and power.

Gudjohnsen: "His speed is what takes him beyond [ordinary] players but his close control is excellent."

Marks: 8/10

Heading ability
Ronaldo is tall and strong and a menace in the air. He would probably score more headers after free kicks if he weren't the one taking most of the free kicks!

Gudjohnsen: "Ronaldo is an incredible threat in the air, his athleticism and speed make him a player you have to watch."

Marks: 8/10

Free kicks
Ronaldo is possibly the most dangerous free kick exponent in the world. He's the master of long-range kicks where the ball suddenly drops into the goal.

Gudjohnsen: "He has scored some incredible free kicks in his career. When he gets it right they are unstoppable."

Marks: 9/10

Team player?
One of Ronaldo's few faults as a player is that he can be egotistic, and will try the impossible shot instead of passing the ball to a teammate who is better positioned. He has, however, improved in this respect in recent years.

Gudjohnsen: "When you have that level of talent, perhaps it is understandable that you think you can do it all?"

Marks: 6/10

Goals
Even though Ronaldo was always talented and skilled, and scored many great goals during his first seasons with United, no one could have imagined that he would become the goal-scoring machine he's turned into with Real Madrid.

Gudjohnsen: "To say one is better than the other [Ronaldo or Messi] is very difficult because the two of them seem very similar in the way they are scoring goals. They are reaching standards that very few of us have seen anyone reach in recent years."

Marks: 10/10!

Ronaldo and Real

When Cristiano Ronaldo joined Real Madrid, Manuel Pellegrini was head coach. Despite raking in points in La Liga, Real came second after Barcelona, and Pellegrini was fired. In his place came José Mourinho, who had won titles with Porto in Portugal, Chelsea in England, and Inter in Italy. He was therefore considered one of the best coaches in the world. He moved Ronaldo from the wings to the front and gave him a free hand (or foot) with fabulous results; Ronaldo flourished and scored goals at a rate almost unheard of in Madrid before.

He was top scorer in Spain during the 2010–2011 season.

Season	La Liga goals	La Liga matches	Matches total	Goals total
2009–2010	29	26	35	33
2010–2011	34	40	54	53
2011–2012	38	46	55	60
2012–2013	34	34	55	55

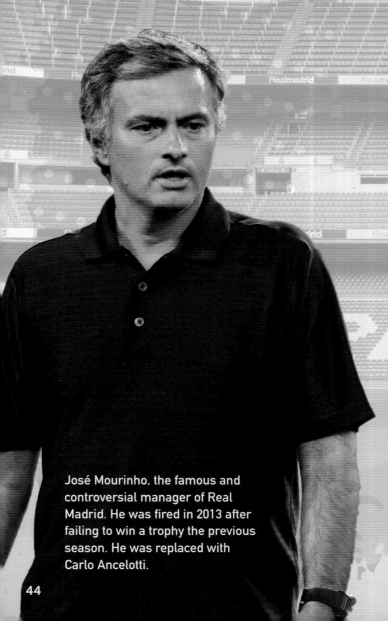

José Mourinho, the famous and controversial manager of Real Madrid. He was fired in 2013 after failing to win a trophy the previous season. He was replaced with Carlo Ancelotti.

Real's performance in La Liga after Cristiano Ronaldo joined:

La Liga 2009–2010

1   Barcelona   99
2   Real   96
3   Valencia   71

UEFA Champions League: Round of 16, lost to the French club Lyon. Inter won the title.

Ronaldo goals in the CL: 7

La Liga 2010–2011

1	Barcelona	96
2	Real	92
3	Valencia	71

UEFA Champions League: Made it to the semifinals but lost to Barcelona, who went on to claim the title.
Ronaldo goals in the CL: 6

La Liga 2011–2012

1	Real	100
2	Barcelona	91
3	Valencia	61

UEFA Champions League: Made it to the semifinals but lost to Bayern München. Chelsea claimed the title.
Ronaldo goals in the CL: 10

La Liga 2012–2013

1	Barcelona	100
2	Real	85
3	Atl. Madrid	76

UEFA Champions League: Made it to the semifinals but lost to Borussia Dortmund. Bayern München won the title.
Ronaldo goals in the CL: 12 (most by any player)

Spanish Champion!

When Cristiano Ronaldo joined Real, he started scoring more than he ever had with United. He played a great part in Real's success. During Ronaldo's first two seasons with Real, the club gathered so many points that at any other time it would have secured victory in La Liga, Spain's top league. But the invincible Barcelona totaled even higher both seasons, and Real had to settle for second place. In the 2011–2012 season, though, no club could touch Real, and Ronaldo scored more goals than ever before. For example, he scored 7 hat tricks!

Real's starting eleven in 2011–2012 usually looked like this:

Casillas

Sergio Ramos – Pepe

Arbeloa   Marcelo

Özil – Alonso – Kaká

Higuaín   Cristiano Ronaldo

Benzema

The midfielder Khedira and the attackers di Maria and Callejón also played a great deal. The coach was the colorful Mourinho.

Constant rivalry with Barcelona

Real Madrid is the most successful soccer club in the world. After the 2012–2013 season, Real had won La Liga 32 times, the Copa del Rey 18 times, and the UEFA European Champions League 9 times.

The club's archrival, FC Barcelona, had won La Liga 22 times, the Copa 26 times, and the UEFA European Champions League 4 times.

The clubs have very different recruitment policies; Barcelona places great stress on home-grown talent, raising its own players from an early age. These boys become the key players in the first team, such as Xavi, Lionel Messi, and Andres Iniesta. Real Madrid, on the other hand, prefers to buy superstars from other clubs and build the team around them—superstars like CRISTIANO RONALDO.

Matches CR7 has played against Barcelona

November 2010–March 2013

	Real wins	Barça wins	Draw	RONALDO goals
La Liga	2	4	2	3
Copa del Rey	2	1	2	5
Super Cup	1	2	1	2
UEFA Champions L.	0	1	1	0

Matches between Real Madrid and Barcelona are called "El Clásico" and are usually very exciting. To begin with, Ronaldo didn't do too well against Barcelona. But on April 21, 2012, that changed. Ronaldo and his Real Madrid teammates turned up at Camp Nou in Barcelona, where Real hadn't managed to win a match in 5 years. But this time Ronaldo scored a winning goal for Real in the 73rd minute, after a great run and an assist from Özil. It was Ronaldo's finest hour. Not only did he secure a victory over the archrivals on their home ground, but he also ensured that Real would be crowned Champions of Spain for the first time since 2008!

The Best!

After Barcelona had won the Spanish premier league three consecutive times, Cristiano Ronaldo and his teammates at Real finally managed to become champions of Spain, 2011–2012.

There were two Portuguese heroes behind Real's success in Spain in the spring of 2012—the coach, José Mourinho, and the superstar, Cristiano Ronaldo! In 2013, Mourinho became head coach of Chelsea for the second time.

CRISTIANO RONALDO
With Real Madrid since 2009

PRIMARY AWARDS

LA LIGA, Spanish premier league 2011–2012

COPA DEL REY, Spanish Cup 2010–2011

SUPER COPA DE ESPAÑA, Spanish Super Cup 2012

TOP GOAL SCORER IN LA LIGA 2010–2011

TOP GOAL SCORER IN THE COPA DEL REY 2010–2011

TOP GOAL SCORER IN UEFA CHAMPIONS LEAGUE 2011–2012

WANTED!

A popular and good-looking soccer player like Cristiano Ronaldo is of course wanted for all sorts of advertising. He earns a lot of money from that kind of work. In this photo, he is promoting a brand of jeans.

10 Facts

Ronaldo's grandmother was from the Cape Verde Islands but moved to Madeira to work as a maid.

In the 2011–2012 season, Ronaldo scored a goal against every team in the Spanish league. That was something no soccer player had achieved before!

Ronaldo's home in Manchester was burgled in 2003 and £30,000 worth of jewelry stolen.

Ronaldo is very interested in fashion and owns his own clothing stores in Lisbon and Madeira, called CR7.

Ronaldo is known for working hard in training, and when he was a teenager he practiced dribbling the ball with weights attached to his ankles. He believed this would make him lighter on his feet in actual matches.

When Ronaldo was 15 he was diagnosed with a racing heart. It could have ended his career; he was already signed with Sporting Lisbon. He was admitted to the hospital, where he underwent laser surgery that went very well. He was back in practice a few days later.

On January 12, 2008, Ronaldo scored his first hat trick for United, when he made 3 goals in a 6–0 victory against Newcastle. On May 5, 2010, he scored his first hat trick for Real in a match against Mallorca.

Ronaldo got his first red card for United on January 14, 2006, for kicking Andy Cole of Manchester City.

Ronaldo's contract with Real states that another club can buy him, whether Real wants to sell or not. But only if that other club is willing to part with 1 billion euros!

Ronaldo has twice scored 4 goals in a single match, both for Real in the 2010–2011 season. His first "double brace" was against Racing Santander in a 6–1 victory, and the second was in a 6–2 victory against Sevilla.

HOW MUCH DOES HE MAKE?

During the 2011–2012 season, Cristiano Ronaldo's monthly salary from Real Madrid was 1.35 million dollars. That is an annual salary of 16 million dollars. But that's not all; like other players he also has additional earnings from bonuses and sponsorship deals.

In 2013, his total earnings were believed to be 40.5 million dollars. It's difficult to figure out the net worth of the top soccer stars in the world, but Ronaldo's net worth is thought to be around 167 million dollars.

It costs 31 million dollars to visit the International Space Station as a tourist. Ronaldo could go every year!

Beluga caviar costs $300 per ounce. Ronaldo could buy 35,000 pounds of it!

Top 10 highest earning players in 2012–13

1	David Beckham, LA Galaxy	$50.6 Million
2	Cristiano Ronaldo, Real Madrid	$43.5 Million
3	Lionel Messi, Barcelona	$40.3 Million
4	Sergio Aguero, Man. City	$20.8 Million
5	Wayne Rooney, Man. United	$20.3 Million
6	Yaya Toure, Man. City	$20.2 Million
7	Fernando Torres, Chelsea	$20.2 Million
8	Neymar, Santos	$19.5 Million
9	Ricardo Kaká, Real Madrid	$19.3 Million
10	Didier Drogba, Galatasaray	$17.8 Million

Serious Car Lover!

Cristiano Ronaldo loves fast luxury cars, and he can afford them. He currently owns 19 cars so he must need a very large garage! Here are a few cars in his collection.

BMW M6

Bentley Continental GTC

Audi R8

Ferrari 599 GTB Fiorano

Rolls Royce Phantom

WHAT NEXT?

Ronaldo's greatest wish had not come true as of 2013, to win the Champions League with Real Madrid. He wants to be the one to bring the elusive tenth Champions League cup to Madrid. If he stays at Santiago Bernabéu there's a good chance that this dream will come true in the end!

Constant rumors link Ronaldo with various big-spending teams in Italy, England, and lately even France. That is only natural. He is one of the greatest soccer players in history, so every ambitious team would of course like to recruit him. He has certainly hinted that one day he might like to return to England or try the climate in Italy, but wherever Cristiano Ronaldo goes, his fans can rest assured that the goals will follow!

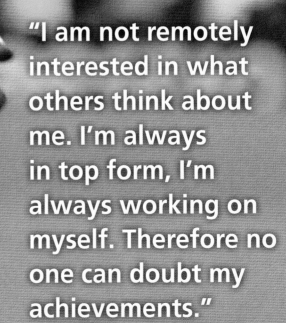

"I am not remotely interested in what others think about me. I'm always in top form, I'm always working on myself. Therefore no one can doubt my achievements."

Learn More!

Books

- *Ronaldo: The Obsession for Perfection*, by Luca Caioli.
  An insightful, well-written, and entertaining biography.
- *Cristiano Ronaldo: An Unauthorized Biography* (e-book), Belmont & Belcourt Books, 2012.
  Comprehensive and full of useful statistics.

Websites

- The **Wikipedia** entry on Cristiano Ronaldo offers an abundance of information about the player, his family, his teams, and his teammates.
- **espnfc.com** (Soccernet)
- **goal.com**
- **101greatgoals.com**
- **realmadrid.com**
- **cristianoronaldofan.com** (A fan page)

Glossary

Striker: A forward player positioned closest to the opposing goal who has the primary role of receiving the ball from teammates and delivering it to the goal.

Winger: The player who keeps to the margins of the field and receives the ball from midfielders or defenders and then sends it forward to the awaiting strikers.

Offensive midfielder: This player is positioned behind the team's forwards and seeks to take the ball through the opposing defense. They either pass to the strikers or attempt a goal themselves. This position is sometimes called "number 10" in reference to the Brazilian genius Pelé, who more or less created this role and wore shirt number 10.

Defensive midfielder: Usually plays in front of his team's defense. The player's central role is to break the offense of the opposing team and deliver the ball to their team's forwards. The contribution of these players is not always obvious but they nevertheless play an important part in the game.

Central midfielder: The role of the central midfielder is divided between offense and defense. The player mainly seeks to secure the center of the field for their team. Box-to-box midfielders are versatile players who possess such strength and foresight that they constantly spring between the penalty areas.

Fullbacks (either left back or right back): Players who defend the sides of the field, near their own goal, but also dash up the field overlapping with wingers in order to lob the ball into the opponent's goal. The fullbacks are sometimes titled wing backs if they are expected to play a bigger role in the offense.

Center backs: These players are the primary defenders of their teams, and are two or three in number depending on formation. The purpose of the center backs is first and foremost to prevent the opponents from scoring and then send the ball towards the center.

Sweeper: The original purpose of the sweeper was to stay behind the defending teammates and "sweep up" the ball if they happened to lose it, but also to take the ball forward. The position of the sweeper has now been replaced by defensive midfielders.

Goalkeeper: Prevents the opponent's goals and is the only player who is allowed to use their hands!

Pick Your Team!

Who do you want playing with Cristiano Ronaldo?
Pick a team for him. Don't forget the coach!

Coach:

_____

Goalkeeper:

_____

Right back:

_____

Left back:

_____

Defender:

_____

Defender:

_____

Midfielder:

_____

Midfielder:

_____

Midfielder:

_____

Striker:

_____

Striker:

Ronaldo

Striker:

9

You transfer to Sporting and are a hit. Go forward 3 places.

11

You make a wrong call and transfer to Liverpool. Go to the ManU place and start from there.

13

You eat too much Bacalao à Brás and miss your turn. Wait 1 round.

Dream come true: you debut with Nacional. Roll again.

6

You're injured after a nasty tackle. Wait 1 round.

You join Andorinha. Go forward 2 places.

You are Cristiano Ronaldo!

The R Boo Gar

You score free-kick g Shout "RONALDO THE BEST three time

Play with 1 die

3

2

Kick off!